We Can Take This City!

We Can Take This City
ISBN 1-888152-00-1
Unless otherwise stated,
Scripture quotations are taken from
the King James Version of the Bible.

Jerry Savelle Ministries International
P.O. Box 748
Crowley, TX 76036
USA
or
Jerry Savelle Ministries International
Kenya National Office
Africa Division Headquarters
P.O. Box 55683
Nairobi, Kenya

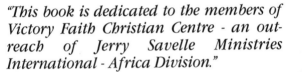

"This book is dedicated to the members of Victory Faith Christian Centre - an outreach of Jerry Savelle Ministries International - Africa Division."

- Dr. Jerry Savelle

God Loves People – He Really Does!

God sees YOU as a potential champion! *Me?* Yes, you. You have a mandate from God. God has called you to spread this Gospel to the world. You might say, "Well, I've done a lot of bad things in my life. What could Jesus possibly want with me?" You're exactly what Jesus died for. You're the reason He died. In fact, Jesus died while you were yet a sinner.

He didn't die when you got better. He didn't die for you when you straightened up your life. He died for you when you were absolutely rotten to the core. But He loved you. That's Agape love. The God kind of love.

It goes beyond human love. Human kind of love is conditional. It says, "I love you if .... you love me. I love you if... you're not mean to me." However, the love of God is unconditional. God loves you ... regardless. No *if's* involved. When there was no hope for us, when we were headed for a devil's hell, Jesus died, shed His blood, and was raised from the dead so that you and I might be justified before Almighty God . The Apostle Paul says that we now have peace with God. God's not mad at you. God doesn't dislike you. God loves you. He desperately loves you. All He asks is for you to love Him.

I want you to notice in Matthew 9:35-38 Jesus' attitude towards people. It says, *And Jesus went about all the cities and villages teaching in their synagogues and preaching the gospel of the kingdom and healing every sickness and every disease among the people. But when he saw the multitudes he was moved with compassion on them, because they fainted and were scattered abroad, as sheep having no shepherd. Then saith he unto his disciples, The harvest truly is plenteous, but the labourers are few; Pray ye therefore the Lord of the harvest, that he will send forth labourers into his harvest.*

When Jesus looks at people, He doesn't just see flesh and blood. He doesn't see black faces, white faces, red faces, yellow faces. He sees people who are potential champions. He sees people who are scattered without direction in their life. And yet, He loves them so much that He says, *Pray that labourers will be sent across their path.*

The Bible reveals to us that it is the will of God that every man be saved and come into the knowledge of the truth. God wants every man to be saved, but who does He want to be a laborer sent into their lives to share the Gospel of Jesus Christ? YOU.

Catch The Vision

Once you catch the vision of seeing people the way Jesus saw them, you'll never be able to look at another person the same way. You'll see them differently. You're not going to be able to stand in the streets of your city and watch the crowds go by and see what you saw before. You're going to see people who need direction. People who need Jesus.

It is vitally important that you catch the vision of what Jesus sees. Catch the vision of how Jesus responds to people and how He reacts to people. He was moved with compassion.

How do you obtain the same vision and spirit of compassion that Jesus had? **You must become a person of prayer.** When the spirit of intercession comes on you, it will cause you to be willing to stand in the gap for the multitudes, the people in your community, the people in your city, and the people in your nation.

You've got to become serious about winning your city for Jesus and absolutely stand toe-to-toe with the devil, and tell him, "You're not taking my city. You're not taking my community. You're not taking my nation. I'll fight you with everything I have, and I just want you to know, devil, I have weapons that are not carnal! They are mighty through God to the pulling down of strongholds. And in case you haven't noticed, devil, God is on my side. You are helpless and hopeless. No weapon formed against me shall prosper. So, you are coming down in Jesus' Name!"

Catch the vision. Catch the vision of what God wants to do. Catch the vision of an entire city being shaken by the power of the living God. I can see it, and it's getting bigger in me all the time. My wife recently said to me, "I'm so full, I'm about to explode!" She said, "My faith has expanded. I can see things now that just a short time ago, looked utterly impossible, but they don't look impossible anymore."

I can see God literally taking cities and nations. How can that happen? By you and me catching the vision and becoming intercessors, and spiritual warriors. By us being willing to stand in the gap. By us letting Satan know that he's not in charge of our city. Catch the vision, become an intercessor, and then become passionate about winning your city!

Leave Your Comfort Zone

Too many Christians today want a comfortable Christianity. They want a comfort zone. They want to just stay where the blessings are. They don't want to make any sacrifices. They don't want to have to extend themselves.

I've heard pastors say, "I wish God would let me leave this city. Oh, I wish God would move me on." One pastor wanted me to pray that God would let him leave. I said, "Why?" He said, "I hate it here, they persecute me all the time. Every time I try to do something, they come against me." I thought to myself, *I'm not praying you'll leave.* I said, "Where do you want to go?" He said, "I wish God would send me to Florida." I thought, *Why, so you can get a tan?* I have news for him, it's not any different in Florida. They've got devils there too.

They've got devils that hate you, persecute you, and will try to run you out of town.

I want you to notice what happened in Luke 4 while Jesus was preaching in the city of Nazareth where he grew up, and how he was treated by the people. The Bible says, *And the eyes of all them that were in the synagogue were fastened on him.* They were looking at Him intently, and then He said, *This day is this scripture fulfilled in your ears.* He was saying to them that what Isaiah prophesied is no longer a promise, it has become a reality. The man Isaiah was talking about was Him - Jesus. Now, you would have thought everybody in that synagogue would have jumped up, shouted and praised God saying, "The Deliverer has come." But they didn't. They grabbed him by the hand, marched him out back, and tried to kill him. In his own home town!

So, He left Nazareth and went to the city of Capernaum. He preached the same message that He preached in Nazareth, but the people in Capernaum loved Him and begged Him not to leave. If you had just left one city that didn't want you and then you find another city that begs you not to leave, you would think, *This is God. Let's camp out here and go no further.* But notice what Jesus said in Luke 4:43, *I must preach the kingdom of God to other cities also: for therefore am I sent.* He would not stay in His comfort zone.

It would appear to be the ideal situation. They loved Him there. Nobody was opposing Him. But when nobody is opposing you, and when nobody is talking bad about you, you may need to do a check up and take inventory, make sure you're in the will of God. You may not be where God wants you.

Somebody once said, "Well, I always thought being in the will of God meant everything would be perfect." If that's the case, then the apostle Paul never got in the will of God because he never had anything perfect. "Well, I believe when it's God, the doors will just open and everything will be smooth." Everywhere Paul went, the door was shut, the demons were standing guard and religious people were determined that he was not going to get in. But Paul would just take his faith, kick the door down and walk in anyway. I like to call him the apostle of confrontation. He was confronted by devils everywhere he went.

If all you're looking for in your Christianity is comfort, then you're probably missing God. Jesus said the Holy Spirit would be your Comforter. That's part of His ministry. The apostle Paul says that He comforts us in all of our tribulations. You're comforted even though you're opposed. You're comforted even though you are under attack. You are comforted, even though everybody's talking ugly about you. Even if people are telling lies, spreading rumors and gossiping about you, you are comforted.

I never look for comfort zones, in fact, I thrive on challenges. It's just another opportunity to prove Jesus is Lord. Another opportunity to prove the Word works!

Another opportunity to prove that if God be for us, who can successfully be against us.

We're Making History

The Amplified Version of Luke 4:43 says, *I must preach the good news of the kingdom of God to the other cities and towns also; for I was sent for this purpose.* Jesus is saying that His very purpose is to preach to the cities. Notice how Jesus looks at cities. He doesn't see buildings. He sees multitudes. He sees people. He sees ethnic groups. He couldn't stay in His comfort zone and not reach all different types of people. He had to fulfill God's purpose for His life. And so do you. You have a purpose from God. You have an assignment from God.

We have entered into a new era. God is going to continue to bless us. God is going to continue to meet our own personal needs, but we can't just come to church, bless one another, prophecy over one another, talk in tongues, sing a few songs and ignore cities. We've got to target cities. Target nations.

God wants cities and nations – that's the era that we're in. The dictionary defines *era* as an event or a date that marks the beginning of a new or important period in the history of something. I just want you to know that we are making history. We have our assignment from God, and it's time to prepare for the harvest. It's time to get ourselves off our mind, and get our minds on others. It's time to get our minds on reaching our own cities for Jesus. You can count on it, when you have a determined purpose for reaching cities and nations with the Gospel of Jesus, God will see to it that every need you have is met far above what you could ever ask or think!

Yes, we've entered into a new era. We're not going to spend all of our prayer time on us anymore. It's time to begin praying and interceding for the people of our cities. We're not going to spend all of our income on just us anymore, we're going to invest in publishing the Gospel to the nations and then the end will come.

God's going to bless us and take care of us. He's going to meet every need in our lives. At the same time, we are going to be so involved in touching other's lives, that we won't even remember our needs and before we can even think about them, God will meet them. It's a new era. We're making history. It's time to target our cities and our nations with the Gospel!

Do It Quickly!

In John 9:4, Jesus said, *I must work the works of him that sent me, while it is day: the night cometh, when no man can work.* Even back then when Jesus was on the earth in the flesh, He sensed an urgency to do what He had to do and do it quickly!

Jesus trained others, reproduced His vision in them, and empowered them to carry out the vision. Then the Apostle Paul comes along, stirred the people up, and got others excited about reaching cities. Today, we're getting stirred and we're going to fulfill Jesus' vision in our generation.

The devil tried to get us off base by becoming so consumed with our own needs that we didn't think much about others. But, God never intended for us to spend the rest of our lives using this precious thing called faith on us and us alone. He's taught us how to use our faith not only so our needs will be met, but also so we can win cities and nations.

God's saying, "OK, you know how to get your needs met now, and you know how to trust Me, you've learned how to walk by faith, you've learned to cast your cares over on Me, now let's get busy doing what you were called to do. Let's reach nations."

The same faith that will put clothes on your back will turn an entire city to righteousness. I can target my faith against sin in a city, just like I've targeted my faith against sickness and disease in my own body. I can target my faith to a nation just like I can target my faith to my own personal finances or my transportation or my housing. I've learned how to believe God for finances. I believed God for my house. I believed God for my transportation. Everywhere you walk on our ministry grounds or in our home, there's a story behind every piece of furniture, a story behind every suit I wear, a story behind every vehicle we drive and how faith produced it. If faith can produce that, then faith can change a nation and bring it into righteousness.

Jesus said, "I have an assignment. I must target cities and that which I have been sent to do, I must do it quickly." Well, we have the same assignment today. God is wanting us to target cities and do it quickly. It's time to come together. We're serving the same God. We're raising up the same banner of Jesus. We're after the same thing and that is — souls.

Can you imagine hundreds and thousands of people being saved and there not being a church in your city big enough to hold them all? That's not too far-fetched to imagine. It's happening right now. That's where we are on God's timetable. God is raising up "mega churches" in our generation.

Invade Every Man's World

It's time that we channel all of our energies, all of our efforts, all of our finances, all of our prayers, and all of our faith into taking cities and entire nations for the kingdom of God. Do you realize that we are so close to the appearing of the Lord Jesus? That's why we must reach our cities and do it quickly! God has been training us up for this time. He wants us to become vessels of the Holy Spirit to carry His presence and His power into the world and make an impact.

Isn't that awesome to think about? You can impact an entire nation. It doesn't matter what kind of occupation you have - whether you work in construction, a bus driver, or a house wife, *you* can impact your city and your nation with the Gospel of Jesus Christ. God wants to use *you*. You just need to be willing.

God not only wants us to go into all the world geographically, but He wants us to invade every man's world. He wants us to invade the political world. God is going to raise up people who are born again, full of the Holy Ghost, full of the Word of God, who will not compromise, and who can't be corrupted and put them in the political arena.

God is going to raise up people who believe in the power of God, who operate in the miraculous, who can't be corrupted, who will remain pure and upright before God, and put them right in the heart of the economic world. He'll put Believers right in the heart of the educational world, and every where else where there is human existence. That's how we win cities!

God's going to raise up some Believers who will become "ministers of finances". They'll be responsible for more money than they ever dreamed of. God's going to give some Believers businesses that are going to be so prosperous that many will ask, *How are you doing it and where are you getting it?* And they'll respond, **My God supplies all my needs according to his riches in glory by Christ Jesus.** Why would God do this? It's very simple: To win cities and nations!

It's time to invade every man's world. God is looking for some faithful people. He's looking for those who won't run when the pressure is on. God is looking for those who cannot be corrupted. Those who will not compromise. Those who are not moved by persecution or opposition. Those who will stand up for what they believe in. It's time to make a quality decision to reach your city. People are going to want what you have – Jesus.

No other people on earth have the opportunity to make the changes that are so desperately needed in society today, than passionate, visionary, committed Believers. And God's expecting us to seize these opportunities now. The Holy Spirit is working mightily stirring the hearts of millions of lost people right now. They don't understand what's happening, but they are beginning to look for answers. They're no longer satisfied. They don't know where to turn, but thank God that's where you and I come in as laborers. God is getting the church ready to reap this vast harvest of souls. He's going to do a quick work!

Is it truly possible for God to do something quickly? I want you to notice Amos 9:13 says, *Behold, the days come, saith the Lord, that the plowman shall overtake the reaper, and the treader of grapes him that soweth seed; and the mountains shall drop sweet wine, and all the hills shall melt.* What is God saying? He's going to accelerate things to the point that the person who is sowing the seed better get out of the way quick, because the moment the seed hits the ground, the reaper will be right behind him because immediate growth and maturity will take place.

He said the sower will be overtaken by the harvester. As quick as he can sow it in the ground, the harvester is right behind him with a combine ready to harvest. Right behind the harvester comes the sower again. Right behind the sower, comes the reaper again. It's no problem for God to accelerate things and He says in Amos that He plans to do it. Hallelujah!

Don't think small any longer. It's time for us to think bigger. It's going to happen right here in your city and in your nation! God is going to accelerate things. The harvest in the days ahead will literally stagger the imagination of man. We've entered into a new era!

YOU Have A Mandate From God!

What is a *mandate*? A *mandate* is an irrevocable order from God which must be fulfilled by the person or persons to whom it is given. It's an irrevocable order from headquarters. God's not going to change His mind about what He wants you to do. And you must be determined that you will not abort God's plan – no matter what the cost.

God has entrusted you to fulfill His plans and purposes for reaching your city for Him. God wants your city; He wants your nation. He has called, chosen, empowered and commissioned us to invade and conquer. Luke 10:1 says, *After these things the Lord appointed other seventy also, and sent them two and two before his face into every city and place, wither he himself would come. Therefore said he unto them, The harvest truly is great, but the labourers are few: pray ye therefore the Lord of the harvest, that he would send forth labourers into his harvest.*

What were they doing? Targeting cities. The most blessed people are those who step out in faith and reach out to their city when no one else seems to be doing anything. Don't wait for someone else to start. You be the pioneer –God is waiting on YOU!

Notice again in Luke 10 after Jesus sent them into the cities, He empowered them to heal the sick and preach the kingdom of God and verse 19 says, *Behold, I give unto you power to tread upon serpents and scorpions, and over all the power of the enemy: and nothing shall by any means hurt you.*

The Spirit of God recently showed me something about this verse that I had never seen quite this way before. This power was given not for just healing the sick but also for pulling down strongholds that hold cities captive. We have the authority to pull them down in Jesus' Name!

Two thousand years ago, when Jesus made His triumphant entry into Jerusalem, the first thing He did when He got into Jerusalem was attack the spirit of corruption that He found there. Do you know where He found it? In the church. Jesus went into the temple of God and cast out them that bought and sold in the temple and said unto them, *It is written, My house shall be called the house of prayer, but ye have made it a den of thieves.*

25

Notice, He did not go to city hall. He found it in the church. The reason city hall is corrupt is because the church is corrupt. So, what did He do? Notice these two terms: Cast out and over throw.

That's our job in our cities. It is time to cast out and over throw every spiritual stronghold that's stopping our city from experiencing the Lordship of Jesus. It starts in the church. Godly standards must be set in the church. More churches are going to be exposed because that which is hidden is going to come to the light. Strongholds are coming down.

When we get the church cleansed, then city hall will be cleansed. That's why Jesus went to the church first, to cleanse it, to cast down, and to throw out the spirit of corruption. We are not going to conform to the world, the secular world nor the religious world. We're going to be lights in a dark world. God is going to use us to bring masses of people into the glorious light of the Gospel.

Determine to change the spiritual climate of your nation with the Word of God. Do it with your upright living. Don't be silent. Don't think small anymore. Think big! Your voice can be heard in your city. Your voice can be heard in your nation. Jesus is expecting us to recover our cities from the grip of every evil force by which it has been controlled. He expects us to preach the Gospel to the poor, to heal the broken hearted, and to set at liberty those that are bruised. Time is running out. It's time to win your city for Jesus!

For those who don't know Jesus, would you like to know Him?

If you were to die today, where would you spend eternity? If you have accepted Jesus Christ as your personal Lord and Savior, you can be assured that when you die, you will go directly into the presence of God in Heaven. If you have not accepted Jesus as your personal Lord and Savior, is there any reason why you can't make Jesus the Lord of your life right now? Please pray this prayer out loud, and as you do, pray with a sincere and trusting heart, and you will be born again.

Dear God in Heaven,

I come to you in the Name of Jesus to receive salvation and eternal life. I believe that Jesus is Your Son. I believe that He died on the cross for my sins, and that You raised Him from the dead. I receive Jesus now into my heart and make Him the Lord of my life. Jesus, come into my heart. I welcome you as my Lord and Savior. Father, I believe Your Word that says I am now saved. I confess with my mouth that I am saved and born again. I am now a child of God.

Dr. Jerry Savelle is a noted author, evangelist, and teacher who travels extensively throughout the United States, Canada and overseas. He is president of Jerry Savelle Ministries International, a ministry of many outreaches devoted to meeting the needs of Believers all over the world.

Well-known for his balanced Biblical teaching, Dr. Savelle has conducted seminars, crusades and conventions for over twenty years as well as holding meetings in local churches and fellowships. He is being used to help bridge the gap between the travelling ministry and the local church. In these meetings, he is able to encourage and assist pastors in perfecting the saints for the work of the ministry. He is in great demand today because of his inspiring message of victory and faith and his accurate and entertaining illustrations from the Bible. He teaches the uncompromising Word of God with a power and an authority that is exciting, but with a love that delivers the message directly to the spirit man.

When Dr. Savelle was 12 years old, God spoke to his heart as he was watching the healing ministry of Oral Roberts on television. God told him that He was calling him into the ministry. Some years later, Dr. Savelle made Jesus Christ the Lord of his life and since that time, has been moving in the light of that calling.

Dr. Savelle is the Presiding Officer of Victory Faith Christian Centre in Nairobi, Kenya and the founder of Overcoming Faith Churches of Kenya. The missions outreach of his ministry extends to over 50 different countries around the world. His ministry also delivers the powerful message of God's Word across the United States through the JSMI Prison Ministry Outreach.

Dr. Savelle is also the founder of the JSMI Bible Institute and School of World Evangelism located in Crowley, Texas. It is dedicated to training students to hear and be led by the Holy Spirit and take the uncompromising Word of Faith into all the world.

Dr. Savelle has authored a number of books and has an extensive cassette teaching tape ministry. Thousands of books, tapes, and videos are distributed around the world each year through Jerry Savelle Ministries.

For a list of tapes, books and
videos by Jerry Savelle, write:

Jerry Savelle Ministries International
P.O. Box 748
Crowley, Texas 76036
or
Jerry Savelle Ministries International
Kenya National Office
Africa Division Headquarters
P.O. Box 55683
Nairobi, Kenya